TALES OF MODERN DATING FAILS

TAMAR TREMAINE

SPARK Publications

Charlotte, North Carolina

Salty Flames
Tamar Tremaine

Designed, produced, and published by SPARK Publications

Published by SPARKpublications.com
Charlotte, North Carolina

Cover illustrations by Tamar Tremaine and
SPARK Publications.
Interior illustrations by Tamar Tremaine.

Marbled texture by BlurryMe / Shutterstock.com

First Edition Paperback, September, 2021,
ISBN: 978-1-953-55510-6
First Edition Hardcover, September, 2021,
ISBN: 978-1-953-55511-3
First Edition E-book, August, 2021, ISBN: 978-0-578-89399-0
Library of Congress Control Number: 2021913635

DISCLAIMER

——————————— ———————————

This book is a work of creative nonfiction based on true events. It reflects the author's present recollections of experiences over time. Memories can be imperfect and fade over time. Names and characteristics have been changed, events have been compressed, and dialogue has been recreated. In a few instances, two stories have been compressed into one. The illustrations are based on real people. Characteristics have been changed, and characters have been shuffled around to help protect the identities of those in the stories. Real people on whom the characters depicted herein are based may have memories conflicting with the author's recollections. This book was not intended to cause harm to any real person. This book is intended to inspire readers to keep trying, and no harm or embarrassment is directed or implied to those that simply were not a fit for the author.

CONTENTS

Jetsetter **53**

Speciman **81**

Lady Killer **61**

Saucebox **89**

Shameplant **69**

Cranberry Vodka **97**

Cranberry Vodka **75**

Swingrich **103**

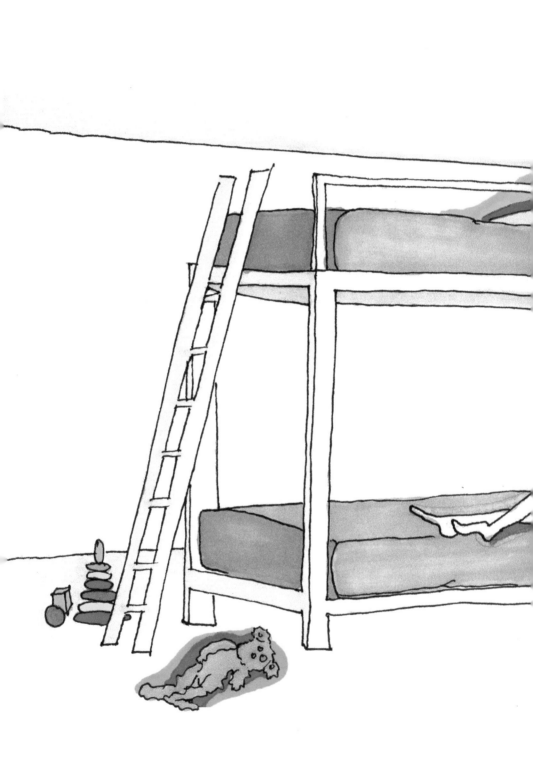

"

WHAT'S THE WORST THAT COULD HAPPEN?

"

TAMAR TREMAINE

Architect/Serial Dater, 32 years old, 0 miles away

Stoic
Petite Brunette
Independent woman
Easy to open up to
Bad at small talk
Kinda shy
Aquarius

ME (TAMAR TREMAINE)

A LITTLE ABOUT ME:

I'm a successful architect who lives in the big city. You can typically find me in black leggings with a fitted shirt and fancy sneakers, trying to show off my body without showing off my body. I'm not photogenic, so everyone online thinks I look better in person. Or maybe that's part of my strategy?

When I'm bored, I go on dates ... a lot of dates. I love meeting people, charming people, and imagining my future life with people. I'm optimistic, and I see the best in everyone. I'm looking for someone who:

♥ Challenges me
♥ Enhances my life
♥ Makes me a priority
♥ Smells good
♥ Is at least OK in bed
♥ Makes enough money to support himself
♥ Is willing to go on adventures with me
♥ Will let me steal his sweatpants

♥ Is taller than 5'5"
♥ Is at least a little attractive
♥ Is willing to cuddle with me

I think my list of requirements is pretty reasonable, but time and again my expectations prove to be too high. Over the years, the stories I've shared about my bad dating life have made a lot of people feel better about theirs. I hope to make you feel better too or maybe even inspire you to put yourself out there. What's the worst that could happen?

"

HEY I THINK I LOST YOUR NUMBER. GIRRRRRRL CAN I GET YO DIGITS?

"

CHALK BOY

Student/Revolutionary, 22 years old, 1 mile away

Ginger-ish
Long eyelashes
Swimmer, Funny, Shy
Dedicated to coaching others
Team player
Leo

CHALK BOY

A RERUN OF THE *Keeping Up with the Kardashians* premier flicks on the television screen. I switch it off immediately. I have no interest in watching rich kids complain about how hard their lives are. I'm halfway through my first year of college. School is a little lonely without my sister, and my best friend has really been there for me. I promised I would go to a party with her, but I have schoolwork to worry about. I need to focus so I can keep my commitment.

Meanwhile, "Chalk Boy" and his friends are hanging out in a dorm across campus. They've had a few too many drinks, and have decided to start a fake revolution. They roam around campus writing "Chalk Boy Revolution" on every surface in sight. There's no story behind the revolution—just a bunch of drunk boys goofing around.

Later, my friend and I leave the party for some fresh air. We see "Chalk Boy Revolution" graffitied on the Social Sciences building, and think it would be funny to cross out "Chalk Boy" and change it to "Tamar Tremaine." My friend takes a photo of me posing in front of our masterpiece.

Later that night, I make the photo my Facebook profile picture. Facebook is this new social networking site that requires you to sign up with a college email address.

A couple of weeks later, Chalk Boy himself adds me as a friend on Facebook. He messages me, "Awesome profile picture, haha." I had forgotten about my new picture. Funny that he found me on Facebook so many days later. He's kind of cute. I don't really have time for dating right now, but I wonder if he finds me attractive.

I message him back. He doesn't respond.

My friend and I start an elaborate inside joke about the future romance between me and Chalk Boy. We get married, buy a house in Texas, and have four kids. We live in a small town, and he uses his campaign experience to successfully run for mayor. It would be pretty crazy to meet my soulmate by crossing out his chalk art and posting it online. He never responds to my Facebook message, and eventually the joke slips from our memories.

After graduation, I move to Los Angeles for grad school. Chalk Boy messages me on Facebook and says,

"Hey dude, how long have you been out here in California? I think I live pretty close by."

We chat back and forth over the next few days and eventually make plans to meet for beers at a bar near his apartment. Dating the famous Chalk Boy is now suddenly a real possibility.

When he arrives, he is flushed with a nervous smile. I take a few easy breaths and look him straight in the eyes. I'm not as nervous as I thought I would be. As we make our way to a table, my shoes stick to the floor of the bar, and the air smells a bit like stale beer—just like college days.

There's an awkwardness hanging in the air. He is waiting for me to kick off the conversation. For someone who wrote his name all over campus, he seems kind of lackluster.

I start off with some basic "get to know you" questions. He tells me about his job as a swim coach and his tiny, old apartment with popcorn ceilings and peeling laminate countertops. I tell him about the struggles of architecture school and my job as a hostess at a diner, where I'm routinely told that I will never be good enough to be a waitress. We reminisce about our undergrad days, and he tells me what it was like to be a college athlete. It's kind of fun learning about someone I don't know and evaluating them as a prospective suitor. After drinks, he kisses me goodnight. I'm a little caught off guard, and it sort of feels like he is slobbering all over my face. There's no passion. No spark.

We hang out a couple more times; however, the chemistry just isn't there. He is amiable but doesn't live up to the Chalk Boy in my head. He rekindles with an ex-girlfriend, and she asks him to stop seeing me. We lose touch.

They must have eventually broken up, because Chalk Boy messages me on Facebook a few years later and says, "Hey I think I lost your number. Girrrrrrl can I get yo digits?"

I roll my eyes, laugh, and send him my phone number. He never texts me.

"
LAST NIGHT
WAS SO FUN,
RIGHT?
"

TEDDY BEAR

Graphic Designer, 25 years old, 9 miles away

Teddy Bear
Tall and muscular
Why is he all alone?
Such a confident dancer
Mysterious

TEDDY BEAR

IT'S MY FAVORITE HOLIDAY: Halloween. I walk down to Main Street from my office to meet two friends for the Pride Parade. It's convenient that my first big girl job happens to be a block away because traffic and parking are usually a nightmare. I work in the gay neighborhood in town, and there is an undercurrent of hope and excitement as New Jersey just became the fourteenth state to recognize same-sex marriages. Progress.

Every year, thousands of people flock to the parade to march down the street in extravagant costumes. It's the place to be on Halloween. Celebrities often make appearances, and every bar and club have a line around the block. My eyes glow as we look in awe at the incredible costumes. We skip through the street, taking a selfie with an avocado and a California roll. We make it to the end of the parade and start assessing cover charges at a few bars. I guess we're too late because they're all crazy expensive.

We see a bunch of people dancing to a DJ in a parking lot. That option looks more budget friendly, so we head over. We start dancing, and a guy walks up. He's all alone, and he's dressed like a giant teddy bear. He's a great dancer. We dance together all night. But just before the music stops, his friend shows up, and they both disappear. We didn't even get to exchange numbers.

When I get home that night, I post a photo of me and my friends on Instagram. I tag the parking lot as our location.

The next morning, I wake up to an Instagram notification. I have a direct message from a username I don't recognize. Most people don't even use the direct message feature. Sliding into someone's DMs doesn't become a thing for another year.

The message is pretty generic: "Hi, how you are?" The profile picture seems familiar... he looks a lot like Teddy Bear. I click his username to see his photos. He's cute, but it's hard to tell if it's him without the fur. There's a photo on his page from the parade, but he's not in it.

I respond with, "Good. So hungover though. How are you?"

He immediately writes back. He says, "Same. Last night was so fun, right?"

Now I'm sure it must be Teddy Bear. I'm late for work, so I have to cut our conversation short.

We continue to message for a few weeks. He tells me that he works as a graphic designer. He moved to Los Angeles because there are so many great creative work opportunities. He's trying to work his way up the ladder and prove to his family that he can make a good living as a designer. He thinks it's awesome that I work in design too, and he thinks I'm very pretty. Eventually, we plan a date.

We meet at a quaint restaurant in an alley I arrive a little early, but the hostess seats me anyway. I look up from my menu. A man with dark straw-like hair and deep sunken eyes walks toward the table. Teddy Bear looks … different. Not like I remember. He looks fragile and a little shorter than I recall. Maybe the costume made him appear stockier? Teddy Bear takes short, jerky steps, and his right hand shakes a little bit.

He stares into the distance and says, "G-g-good day."

I smile at him, hoping to boost his confidence, and say, "Hi! What did you get up to this weekend? It's nice to meet you again!" He responds with a blank, confused stare.

After about fifteen minutes of awkward attempts at conversation, I realize that he is not Teddy Bear, and he does not understand English very well. I'm typically confident on first dates, but I start to get nervous too. Did he just message a bunch of random girls in the area hoping to find an after after-party? How did I get myself into this situation? His English seemed fluent on direct message. Why is he struggling to understand me?

The table is lit with a real candle with an open flame. With my mind on other things, I don't notice my menu slipping down, closer and closer to the candle, until it's suddenly in flames. Everyone at the restaurant is staring at me. The waiter calmly walks over and hands me a new menu, as if I'm not the first. I start thinking up excuses to leave.

"TUVE UN GRAN TIEMPO.

"

CHILAQUILES
Graphic Designer, 25 years old, 0 miles away

Nice guy
Cute
Eager to impress
Sliding into DMs before it was cool
Shy IRL
Aries

CHILAQUILES

The date continues.

AFTER MY INITIAL moment of panic, I decide to order food and proceed with the date. He's very polite, and he was interesting over DM. Maybe his language skills are suffering because he is so nervous. I use small words and speak slowly. We struggle through some basic conversation for the next hour.

He tells me about his goals as a designer and about how he moved here recently from Venezuela. He doesn't know many people yet. I think back to when I first moved here. It took me a long time to make a good group of friends. I felt very lonely for the first few months.

He does a decent job finding words to tell me about himself, but as soon as I start to speak, he squints his eyes in concentration, and his brows draw together. He asks me what a lot of words mean. I begin to feel socially exhausted. I don't speak any Spanish. I tell him I'm tired, and we pay the bill and head home.

Later that night, my phone lights up. I have a direct message from Chilaquiles. He says that he had a great time and asks if we can hang out next weekend. I have to think about it. I don't respond.

The next morning, I click open my Instagram and stare at Chilaquiles' message. He was sweet and friendly, and I know what it feels like to move to a big city where you don't know anyone. I think, *maybe we can watch a movie, then we don't have to talk as much.* I tell him that I would love to hang out next weekend.

Chilaquiles arrives. I don't own a TV, so I propose that we watch a movie on my laptop. I share a loft in the city with a of couple friends, and given our small paychecks, buying a TV hasn't exactly been a priority. Chilaquiles and I sit down to watch, but instead of watching, he attempts to have a conversation. He talks through the entire movie.

My jaw is clenched, and I start to get a headache. He still can't understand much of what I'm saying. I get frustrated. Then I feel bad for being frustrated. He just moved to a new country. It's going to take him time. Still, I don't want to be the one to help him learn, and I hate myself for it. I tell him I need to get to bed because I have to work the next day.

We continue talking on Instagram for a couple of weeks, but eventually I stop responding.

"
I PAID FOR THESE, SO THESE ARE MINE.
"

SNEAT DETECTOR

Nepotist, 27 years old, 15 miles away

Beach boy
Curly brown hair
Surfer accent, broad arms
Working hard to one day hardly work
Calls every day

SNEAT DETECTOR

I'M LATE MEETING Sneat Detector for our fifth date. He dropped me a pin for a location with free parking, and I've been driving around trying to find the lot for thirty minutes. I had to work late, and I'm hangry. He keeps calling me, wondering where I am. So far, all of our dates have been food and drinks at public locations, just the two of us. Today we're taking it up a notch. He's introducing me to his friends.

I eventually give up trying to find the free parking lot, and I park in a paid lot. I get out of my car, and I walk over to the marina to meet him and his friends. I'm surprised to see him standing all alone.

He says, "Kitty, I don't know what we're going to do now. My friends got tired of waiting and left." He always calls me Kitty. It's so strange. I'm starving, so I propose that we grab food nearby. He chooses a restaurant up the street.

We plant ourselves in a booth, both on the same side. I always sit on the same side of the booth as my dates. It often weirds guys out until they realize that I'm perfectly located for a quick brush of the leg or some spoon feeding. Just kidding. I would never let a guy spoon feed me. I'm very soft spoken and prefer to sit closer because I'm tired of repeating myself over and over in response to, "WHAT!? What did you say?"

The server walks up, and I order a burger and a beer. He only orders a beer. I crinkle my brow. "Aren't you going to get food too? I don't want to be the only one eating."

"We can share your burger." Before the server can walk away, he says, "Can I get the check?"

Who does that? Who asks for the check before the food comes out?

Sneat Detector flips open his wallet and starts counting one-dollar bills. My stomach tenses up. He must not have ordered food because he can't afford to spend any more money on our date. I've asked him about what he does for work a few times, and he's always a bit vague. I still don't understand exactly what his job is.

The awkwardness subsides. He tells me about how recreational pot was recently legalized in Colorado and his little brother's ice bucket challenge video. The server brings out our beer and half burgers and the check. Sneat Detector begins to fill in the receipt. "Hey, do you have $5.00 for the tip by chance?"

Caught off guard, I realize that I left my wallet in the car. It wasn't intentional. I was in a bit of a frenzy since I drove around lost for so long. I bounce my knee and meekly mutter, "Oops, I think I left my wallet in my car. I don't have any cash on me." I swallow a couple sips of beer, and then take a bite of my half burger. I pick up my beer glass to take another sip, and just as it's tilted up to my mouth, he pulls it away from me. As he pulls it away, beer spills all over the front of my shirt. He takes away my half burger as well.

He raises his brows and says quite sternly, "I paid for these, so these are mine. I'm not here to provide random girls on Plenty of Fish with free dinner."

We'd been on a few dates, so I thought we were past the stage where I could be considered "random." I didn't mean to give him the impression that I was using him for free food. I guess I could have offered to pay, but I've never paid for dinner before. I grew up in the South, and men always go out of their way to pay for things. I feel a bit awkward even offering. I don't want to diminish his manliness. This is so cringeworthy. What do I say now?

"I'm so sorry. I'm not using you for free food. I really do want to get to know you. Next time I will pay."

He gives me a sideways glance and says, "You seem to be avoiding coming over." In a flat tone.

With downcast eyes, I say, "Well, last date I did avoid coming over. It was that time of the month, and I had bad cramps. I don't really feel comfortable having sex for the first time on my period."

He sighs, "It would have been fine. I have towels."

This date keeps getting more awkward.

Clearing my throat, I say, "I'm sorry. I didn't feel comfortable."

"I'm going to take you back to your car. I think we should stop seeing one another. I just don't think we're vibing."

I sigh, relieved. He takes me to my car, and I head home. That wasn't how I expected the date to end, but I think I may have dodged a bullet.

"

YOU HAVE CEMENTED YOUR SPOT IN THE HALL OF DISAPPOINTING PEOPLE.

"

CYBERSTALKER

Personal Trainer, 28 years old, 4 miles away

Italian
Tall, dark, handsome
A little crazy, though
Refuses to take no for an answer
Optimistic

CYBERSTALKER

CYBERSTALKER TEXTS to say he's just walked into the lobby of my apartment building. I close out the photo of a gold and yellow dress that I'm looking at and grab my things to head down. I'm pretty nervous, because he's only the fourth Tinder date I've ever been on. I tried a few other apps, and it didn't go so well. I'm hoping the quality will be better on Tinder.

I live downtown, and it's hard to get friends to visit because they don't want to pay for parking, so I've resorted to trying to meet people on Tinder. My friends and I are all still early in our careers, struggling our way up the ladder. Cyberstalker doesn't live downtown but a lot of his clients do, so he's often in the area.

I hop out of the elevator. He's much taller than I was expecting. He's in amazing shape ... he is a personal trainer after all. We're going to go swimming at a rooftop pool a few blocks away.

When we arrive, he flashes a badge to the doorman. I recognize the building because there's a rumor that a celebrity purchased the entire penthouse level. The doorman lets us up to the pool, which happens to be on the penthouse level.

The pool feels very fancy. There are a few nicely shaded lounges, and it's not crowded. There's also a great view of the city. We swim for a bit and then lounge in the sun. Cyberstalker seems nice, but I just don't feel a spark. I find myself getting annoyed at little things he says and does.

He asks if I want to see his client's place. Curiosity gets the best of me, and I say "Sure!" We head down the hall, and when we get to the door, he just lets himself in. It's a little odd that he has a key.

I start to feel uncomfortable as we walk inside the penthouse despite its beauty. What if his client comes home? Won't he be weirded out that we let ourselves into his place? Cyberstalker offers me a drink and heads to the kitchen. I can smell Aesop Resurrection.

I hear a key in the lock. The knob turns, and the celebrity walks in! He's surprised to see us yet tries to play it cool. Cyberstalker clearly didn't tell him that we were stopping in. My face turns beet red, and I glance around for an escape. The celebrity makes polite conversation for a few minutes, and before things can get any worse, I tell Cyberstalker I need to head home.

He insists on walking me to my apartment. When we get there, I don't want him to come up, but I also don't know how to politely tell him no. He walks me up and then invites himself in.

Ugh. He's making himself comfortable.

I sit and talk with him for thirty minutes or so and then tell him that I really need to clean my apartment and run a few errands. He says he can hang out while I clean, nodding and smiling. He doesn't want to leave. I am now frustrated. I don't want to be mean, but I really want him gone. I finally tell him, with a stern voice, that I will walk him out.

Cyberstalker texts me and tells me that he had a really good time. He asks me out to dinner later in the week. I stare at his text message. I'm not sure what to say. I bite the inside of my cheek. I don't want to go out to dinner with him, but how do I tell him no nicely? What if I hurt his feelings or make him feel bad about himself? I continue to fixate on his text.

The next evening, he texts me again. I still haven't replied to his first text.

He says "Hi, how was your day?" and then sends me a flexing selfie.

I stare at his text. I'm not sure what to say. Turns out I don't have to say anything. He is perfectly capable of maintaining a conversation all by himself.

He says, "My day was great!" and then tells me about the clients he worked with that day.

He keeps texting me. I have to respond. What do I have to say for him to get the hint? I finally work up the courage to tell him that I had a nice time and thought he was a great guy, but I do not wish to go on another date.

He retorts right away, telling me that I have, "cemented my spot in the hall of disappointing people." He says that I'm just like every other girl—I'm selfish, I lead people on, and I play childish games. His complete overreaction to my text tells me that I made the right decision. I click my phone off and place it upside down, missing his next five text messages.

Over the course of the next couple of weeks, he continues to text me. I do not respond. He checks in with me almost every day, sending updates on the status of his arm muscles. I have never blocked anyone before, yet I wonder if I should start.

A few months go by, and I'm on a date with someone else out of town. We have just finished watching the races, and now we're at a free concert on the lawn outside the racetrack. He's standing behind me with his arms around my waist when my phone vibrates. I look, and a full nude video of Cyberstalker playing with himself fills my entire screen. I'm so embarrassed that I quickly put my phone in my back pocket, but I'm positive that my date saw the video.

Later that night, I block Cyberstalker. My phone vibrates. I have a Facebook message from Cyberstalker. He sent me a heart eyes emoji and, "How are you?"

I do not respond.

My phone vibrates again. Another message from Cyberstalker. It's a dog with heart eyes. I do not respond. My phone vibrates a third time. Surprise! It's Cyberstalker. He sent me a GIF of one dog giving another dog a massage. I do not respond. Then he sends me a video of what he is watching on TV. I do not respond.

Cyberstalker messages me again, "Wanna go on a hike some time?"

I block him on Facebook.

A month later, I'm working on a big project at work. It's been a while since I've thought about Cyberstalker. My phone vibrates. I have a friend request from him. He must have created a new Facebook account. He sent me a message of a dog with heart eyes. I do not respond.

A few weeks go by, and then Cyberstalker sends me a video of one dog licking another dog. I block his new account. What's with the dog stuff?

Another month later, I'm checking my email, and notice that I have a friend request from Cyberstalker on LinkedIn. Ugh.

Cyberstalker just requested to follow me on Map My Run.

Cyberstalker just requested to follow me on Snapchat.

Cyberstalker just liked 27 of my Instagram posts. 28. 29. Help.

"MY DIVORCE WAS FINALIZED LAST MONTH."

EXMO

Financial Manager/Actor/Rockstar, 27 years old, 1 mile away

Affable
Former Mormon
Searching for his identity
Tries something new every day
Overwhelming
Gemini

EXMO

IT'S A WEIRD TIME in my life. I just arrived home from undergoing major surgery. When I got mad at my boyfriend for not visiting me in the hospital, he broke up with me. Also, I was laid off for missing work while I recovered, which I'm pretty sure is illegal. I've only been out of school for a year, and my salary was barely livable, so I have zero savings. Here I am, still recovering, writing ten cover letters a day. Sometimes, all you can do is keep on keeping on.

After three straight days of writing cover letters, I'm starting to feel a little better. I'm tired of sitting around at home. Maybe I'll re-download Tinder.

I swipe for a couple of nights and finally match with a cute guy. His name is Exmo, and he's a financial manager. I wonder if he will still like me when he finds out I'm unemployed?

We talk for two days, and then he invites me to come over. Conveniently, he lives in the building next door. His building is owned by the same company as mine, and it's almost a replica. It's kind of creepy.

He opens the door, and he's cuter in person! His hair is long and brown, and he has a great smile. He's on a work call. He sounds so confident on the phone ... like he's twenty years older than he actually is.

After he hangs up, he orders dinner: rice bowls from this amazing Korean place up the street. We eat, and then he gives me a back massage and tells me that I'll find a great job. I should hang out with him more often. I have a jittery feeling of excitement as I walk back home.

It's a few days later, and I look Exmo up on Google. I find an article that his company published about him a few months ago. It mentions his dog and his... wife? Is he still married? Did he just get a divorce?

When I interrogate him about it, he tells me that he was married for a year and got divorced a month ago. She took the dog. He grew up Mormon, so it was common in his town to get married young since sex is not allowed until marriage. When he filed for divorce, he also left the Mormon church. His family excommunicated him.

My legs suddenly feel weak, so I sit down. It's kind of a lot to take in at once. A month is not that much time. I wonder if he still has any of his ex-wife's things in his apartment.

Over the next week, it dawns on me that he has a considerable way to go on his post-Mormon journey. I'm with him when he drinks alcohol for the first time. He only has one beer. Baby steps.

One night, we're relaxing on the couch talking, and he mentions that his ex-wife is the only person he has ever had sex with. I suddenly feel so much pressure. It's like I'm hanging out with someone who's still in college. If he's only had sex with one person, what is he expecting from me?

We grab coffee, and it's his first time ever consuming caffeine. He asks if it's normal for his hand to feel shaky. I tell him he'll get used to it.

Everything is a first for him. He looks at the world with the eyes of a child. He wants to experience everything, cut ties with innocence, and become someone new. He even gets new clothes and a haircut to totally change his look. I like the old Exmo, but will I like the new Exmo?

A month later, I'm walking around downtown with Exmo and two of his new friends. There's an art crawl, and they want to get high before we look at art. I'm not a huge fan of weed, but Exmo wants to try it since he's never done it before.

His new friends frequently partake in recreational drugs, are covered in tattoos, and wear a lot of leather. They're friendly, yet it feels a bit like Exmo is having an identity crisis, and I'm not sure how I feel about it. I don't think he knows who he is anymore. I certainly don't. I wonder to myself if I should continue seeing him.

Eventually, everything Exmo does irks me. I'm not sure why. Every time he gets close to me, I feel like I need air. He is generous with his time, energy, and money, and I really appreciate it; yet when I don't return the favor in the way he thinks I should, he gets upset with me, like we're keeping score.

The last straw is when he leans in to give me a kiss with a huge cold sore on his mouth. Right as his face is nearing mine, I notice it and freak out. He could give me herpes! What's he thinking? I tell him he needs to finish his post-Mormon journey on his own. Maybe someday we could try again, but now just isn't the right time.

"
NO PHONES ALLOWED ON A FIRST DATE.
"

CRANBERRY VODKA

Medical Marijuana Consultant, 27 years old, 3 miles away

Uninhibited
Travel addict
Can always make me laugh
Only friends with the cool kids
Momma's boy
Sagittarius

CRANBERRY VODKA

HE'S LATE for our first date. He put on a huge show about planning it but then called the hour before, trying to reschedule. I had moved my plans around in order to accommodate his schedule and insisted that if the date didn't happen tonight, it wouldn't happen ever. Now, here I am, pacing in front of the restaurant. I've never learned the art of patience. Should I have just let him cancel?

He calls to tell me that he's out front, and my flustered pacing has landed me two blocks away. He grumbles about me being late. I speed walk back, a bit flushed, catching my breath. He's wearing a branded polo and backwards baseball cap. Prep meets bro? I guess he is from the East Coast. I kind of have a thing for bros anyways.

We are seated at a table in the middle of a nearly empty restaurant. He orders a cranberry vodka, and I order a stout beer. He loves that. He texts a picture of his pink drink next to my black beer to all of his friends with the caption, "Guess which one is mine?" Then he flips his phone upside down and says, "No phones allowed on a first date."

He goes on to tell a bunch of jokes that don't make any sense. He's so convinced that they are funny that I can't help but laugh. We banter about Brexit but avoid talking about Trump becoming president. You never know how people may have voted these days. When it's time to pay, I plop my card down to split the bill. I sure learned that lesson the hard way. Always offer to pay. He picks up my credit card and throws it across the room to make a grand gesture about being the one to pay. He's got me—I'm a sucker for charming men. Blushing and highly amused, I go and fish my credit card out from under a nearby table.

While driving him home, I tell him that everyone asks me on a second date. Yes, you read that right—I drove him home. He says that I'll be asking *him* on a second date. He's sure of himself when he kisses me goodnight. He grabs the back of my neck and pulls me toward him. I can still feel the sensation of his hand on my neck as I drive away. I shiver.

The next day, he texts, "Did you tell all of your friends how great our date was!?"

A few days later, he asks me on a second date. Tamar leads one-nil!

We go on several dates, and eventually the fateful moment transpires—I sleep with him. I see him without a hat on for the first time. He's starting to go bald. Got to watch out for those men who have hats on in every photo. I'm still attracted to him, but he immediately loses respect for me. I vow never to sleep with him again.

Three days go by, and Cranberry Vodka abruptly calls me late at night, very drunk, asking if I'll drive him home from a nearby bar. I initially tell him no. I'm not his Uber. He insists he called because he wants to see me and offers to buy me dinner on the way home. I give in and drive over.

I have to enter the bar to find him, and he grabs my body like he owns me. I don't like it. I jerk away, feeling a little dizzy. I leave upset, vowing to stop talking to him.

"IT'S HIM! HE'S ON OUR FLIGHT!"

JETSETTER
Flight Attendant, 28 years old, 5,551 miles away

Dutch
Travel Lover
Introverted, Humble
Looking for the next adventure
Tall

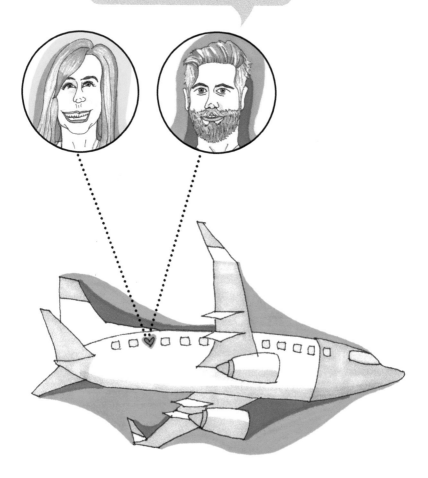

JETSETTER

——————————————— ——————————————

WE JUST WALKED through the sliding glass doors to the International terminal at the airport. My friend and I are flying to Germany for a ten-day vacation. I got promoted at work, and now I have extra vacation time. Plus, we could use a break from breaking news about President Trump's tweets. We're meeting another friend of mine in Germany. The woman at check-in is giving us a hard time because I didn't include my friend's middle name when I booked our flights. I'm trying to talk her into looking past it.

A group of flight attendants walks by us. I lock eyes with one of them. He's tall, with a strong jawline and sharp features, but his smile is soft. I can hear his Dutch accent from across the lobby. He holds my gaze for what seems like forever, and then I break it and return to begging the woman at check-in to let us through.

After we promise for the fiftieth time not to make the same mistake again, the woman at the counter updates my friend's boarding pass and checks our bags. We wind our way through airport security to our gate.

It's finally our turn to board the plane. We walk on.

"It's him! He's on our flight! Did I just say that really loudly? Oops." My pulse is beating rapidly, and my eyes gleam.

We take our seats, and I remove my shoes and get comfortable, setting up my pillow and blanket. I'm great at sleeping on planes.

While I'm fast asleep, Jetsetter drops a note and a couple pieces of chocolate in the chair pocket in front of me. The note says, "You're really pretty" with his Instagram handle and WhatsApp.

I wake up from my nap. Jetsetter stops by and asks me if I liked my chocolate. I don't know what he's talking about, but I smile madly and tell him it was great.

When he leaves, I turn to my friend, "He talked to me!" My friend tells me to look in my chair pocket. I get a rush of adrenaline.

We have a layover in Amsterdam. After we exit the plane, I text Jetsetter. He asks if I want to meet him for coffee at an airport café´ We sit at a small table next to a large glass wall. My friend leaves to entertain herself and secretly films our airport date through the glass.

Jetsetter tells me that he lives in Amsterdam. He became a flight attendant a couple of years ago because he loves to travel, although sometimes he gets tired of living out of hotel rooms. His career also makes dating difficult. Maybe a relationship with me could work. After all, I do live in a city that happens to be a major hub for his airline.

I stare into his gray eyes and contemplate how beautiful our children would be. It seems he's not used to people gushing over him despite how tantalizing he is. Maybe Amsterdam girls don't find him as attractive for some reason? I think he's beautiful.

He walks me back to meet my friend for our next flight. To my surprise, she invites Jetsetter to come stay with us at our Airbnb in Germany. He laughs and kisses me goodbye.

When our flight lands in Germany, I have a message from him. It says, "Maybe I will come stay with you in Germany. Let me look up flights."

The next day, I hear a knock on the door at our Airbnb. Jetsetter is here! I can't believe he flew to Berlin to spend time with me. I can't stop smiling.

He turns out to be a great addition to the group. He gets along well with everyone, and he's happy to go along with our plans. I feel so comfortable and secure around him. We spend an entire day exploring the city. I wonder if he could be the one and then tell myself I'm being ridiculous. I'm getting caught up in the moment. We barely know each other.

Our feet start hurting, so we stop at one of those spas where fish eat all the dead skin off your feet. It's super touristy, but you only live once, right? Jetsetter is in the tank next to me. He's perfect. I wish there were guys back home like him. I could settle down with someone like him. The fish keep tickling my feet.

We follow with happy hour, dinner, and dancing. Jetsetter is sure to take care of me when I drink too much. We share a bed, yet he doesn't pressure me to move too quickly. I feel so lucky and special.

We spend the next couple of days together, and then he has to fly back home for work. I'm devastated to see him go. My heart hurts. I get a little teary-eyed as he calls for a taxi.

As he's walking out the door to get in his taxi, he gets a phone call from his son. Wait, what? He calls from the airport to explain that he was never married, but he got a girl pregnant in high school. He typically has his son two days a week. Dream boy is suddenly seeming less dreamy. He also tells me, full disclosure, that he lives at home with his parents.

It seems I may have put Jetsetter up on a pedestal in my head. I like the idea of him better than the real him. I want to marry someone who doesn't have any kids. I guess what happens in Germany stays in Germany.

"
DO YOU THINK IT'S SAFE FOR US TO DRIVE HOME?
"

LADY KILLER
Trader, Finance, 30 years old, 34 miles away

Long hair
No cares, bad boy
Lots of toys, lots of cash
Always on the run from someone
Delicate
Cancer

LADY KILLER

I HOP OUT OF my Uber just as Lady Killer is pulling up on his motorcycle. He's wearing a leather jacket that doesn't quite hide his tattoos. He's very good looking, with a full head—and face—of soft flowing hair.

He parks, and we head up to the roof of the building, where there is a trendy outdoor bar and restaurant with a spectacular view of the city. It's a perfect day. The afternoon sun warms my skin as a soft breeze rattles the nearby palm trees. The air smells like salt and pink jasmine.

We sit down in the last empty booth as he nervously fidgets with his hair and wipes his hands on his pants. He tells me that this is his second online date ever. His first date had misleading photos, and he left disappointed.

The server comes by our booth, and I order a beer, chips, and guacamole. Lady Killer orders a beer and a shot of whiskey. It was his idea to meet at a bar, yet he confesses after ordering that he doesn't really drink anymore. I think the additional shot of whiskey is a little aggressive for 3 p.m., but he seems a little shy. He must be hoping to calm his nerves.

We sit up on the roof for a few hours, having good conversation and a few too many drinks. I feel an unexplainable chemistry even though it's a pretty basic first date. We decide to go out on a second date before the first date is even over. He waits for me in the lobby as I call my Uber home and then takes off on his bike into the setting sun.

A week later, I'm behind Lady Killer on his motorcycle, clutching his jacket for dear life as he flies through residential streets, swerving around anything and everything in his path. He'd mentioned that he picked his first online date up on his motorcycle, and I told him it wasn't fair—I wanted to ride his motorcycle too. Now I'm praying it isn't my last day on Earth. I had no idea that he would be such a crazy driver!

He makes up an excuse to drop by his place on the way to lunch. We park in his parking deck and walk up a flight of stairs to his place. To my surprise, we walk into a two-story flat with an ocean view from both levels. It's relatively clean, well decorated, and there are toys everywhere. There's a case full of guns, three motorized skateboards, a surfboard, a guitar, and a couple of skim boards. He's trying to show off his nice place, but my big takeaway is that he lives in a man cave.

I try to ride one of his electric skateboards and immediately fall on my butt. He's disappointed ... he was hoping I would surprise him and be a skater girl. We put the skateboard away and continue on our way to beer and fish tacos.

The tacos are delicious, and we spend most of the date chatting with the bartender who is very bored. Shortly after we finish eating, he gives me a ride home. He's going to a heavy metal concert with a friend. No kiss goodbye—just an awkward hug.

A week later, I hop in my car and start the engine. Lady Killer wants me to drive sixty miles east for dinner so that I can meet his brother and his brother's girlfriend. I'm not excited about the long trip, but it seems important to him.

I park outside the restaurant. I'm a little hangry. I walk inside, and the server tells me that it's an hour wait for a table. I can't wait that long. I secure a spot for all of us at the bar.

Lady Killer walks in with his brother and company, and they all join me. He pulls out his phone and starts responding to emails. I introduce myself to his brother and his brother's girlfriend. They are both nice although a bit socially awkward.

Lady Killer continues to answer emails for the next hour. I find it quite rude that he has spent the entire date on his phone and left me to fend for myself after I drove so far to see him, but it's 2017. Everyone is glued to their phones. The era of deleting social media to find oneself is not yet upon us. I decide to give him another chance. Everyone makes mistakes, and it's sweet that he wanted me to meet his brother ... right?

We all walk out of the restaurant together, and Lady Killer and I are left standing in the parking lot; just the two of us, unsure what to do next. We both live far from the restaurant, and we don't want to drink anymore because we both have to drive home. We end up making out in his car like two high schoolers. Finally, our first kiss. He's a timid kisser, like he's afraid he might scare me away. I'm puzzled.

I'm accustomed to men being more assertive. I stare into his eyes, hoping for more. My belly flutters. We both break away, and I hop out and head home.

It's the following weekend. I exit the freeway and drive to a bar in the heart of downtown. Lady Killer and I decided to meet there for a drink and then figure out a plan for the rest of the day. Even though our last date didn't go swimmingly, I want to believe that he is more interesting. He hasn't opened up to me yet. After all, we barely know each other.

When I pull up, he tells me that he needs to pick up a check from his moms' house, which is forty-five miles away. It's urgent. He rode downtown on his motorcycle, so it makes more sense for me to drive us both. Or maybe I'm his personal Lyft driver for the day?

He proposes that we get dinner and see a movie at a theater near his mom's house. I reluctantly agree. We have a romantic dinner at Buffalo Wild Wings in the local strip mall along with a couple of beers and then head to the theater.

We park and head toward the box office. As we get close, Lady Killer starts walking in the opposite direction. I grit my teeth, perplexed. We walk toward an older man who is holding two tickets out in front of him. He is standing next to a woman wearing a leather jacket who looks about twenty years younger than him. My muscles tense as I realize that the older man is Lady Killer's dad, and the woman is his new girlfriend. I wave hello and shake my head "no" at the same time. Should I be flattered or concerned?

Lady Killer does not introduce me, and about five minutes in, I just introduce myself. Even with ample time and opportunity in the car, Lady Killer hadn't mentioned that his dad would be joining us. If he had, I might not have agreed to come.

After an awkward hour-and-a-half in the dark, Lady Killer and I leave the theater and head to a bar nearby for one more drink. Well, in his case, another shot and a drink. We still need to pick up the check from his mom's house.

When we finally get to his mom's house, it's late. It's dark and quiet inside. Lady Killer says, "Maybe we should stay here tonight. Do you think it's safe for us to drive home? I'm not sure I should be riding my bike this late. We can sleep in my old room. It's my stepbrother's now, but he's with his dad."

I don't want to stay the night, but I also don't want him driving his motorcycle drunk, so I agree. We walk upstairs to his old room, which has a twin-size bunk bed. His stepbrother's play toys are scattered across the floor. I'm super weirded out. I wonder how far away his mom's room is.

He takes off all of his clothes except his boxers, and lays down on the bottom bunk. I walk toward the ladder to head to the top bunk, and he says, "Aren't you going to cuddle with me?"

Despite my discomfort about the situation, I'm still attracted to him. My mind races. What do I do?

I settle onto the little bed next to him, a little cramped, and try to relax. At this moment, after only one kiss, in his childhood bed, he decides it's time to skip second base and take it to third. He takes my hand and rests it on his shaft. As soon as my skin touches his he immediately comes.

He leaves to take a shower. There is no fifth date.

"

ONLY
MILDLY
DISTURBING.

"

SHAMEPLANT

Director, 35 years old, 2 miles away

Catfish-ish
Sensitive, nice
Photos from ten years ago
That receding hairline tho
Funny
Aquarius

SHAMEPLANT

TYPICALLY, I'm that girl that guys stop talking to three messages in because I'm too boring. I can have fun, don't get me wrong. I'm just not great with witty text banter. But my conversation with Shameplant is effortlessly flowing. We've been messaging back and forth for hours.

When we finally exchange numbers, I save him in my phone as "Guy Who is Actually Funny." He saves me as "Cinderella Draws Buildings." It's a really simplified interpretation of what I do, but come on, it's kind of cute when a guy texts you saying, "HEY. Draw some good buildings today."

After almost a week of that, Shameplant finally asks me on a date. We're going to get sushi. I'm so excited! I'm falling for him, and I haven't even met him yet. And then...

"I need to send you some uglier pictures of me before Tuesday. Here's one."

As it turns out, Shameplant's Tinder photos are about ten years old. He is bald, overweight, and sleep deprived, judging from the bags under his eyes. Should I cancel the date?

He sends me three more photos. My heart sinks further with every photo. Should I give him a chance? Am I judging him too much on his appearance? Maybe we would have a great time together. Maybe he would still make me laugh.

I opt to call Shameplant out for posting old photos on his dating profile. He says he thinks it's unreasonable for me to expect that every photo someone takes will be attractive. He tells me to send him bad photos of me.

I can't argue with that! I decide to keep the date and text Shameplant a bunch of terrible photos. He says, "I would definitely buy that girl sushi."

When I walk into the restaurant, Shameplant is already sitting down, sipping on a glass of water. We start chatting, yet our banter via text doesn't really translate to real-life conversation. Sweat starts to collect on Shameplant's forehead. I wonder if I should have just canceled.

In an effort to learn a little about what he likes to do for fun, I ask Shameplant if he has a lot of friends in town. His eyes well up with tears, and his shoulders slump down. He got in a huge fight with his best friend a couple days ago, and he's pretty sure that their friendship is over for good. He says he doesn't want to talk about it and excuses himself to go use the restroom.

When he returns, his eyes are still red and moist. I stare at my uneaten sushi. I have just made a grown man cry on a first date. What do I do now? Why didn't I cancel? I make a few bad jokes, finish the meal, and then craft an excuse to leave before he can order dessert.

A few days later, Shameplant asks me on a second date. I send him a meme with my face on a piece of toast. He says, "Only mildly disturbing." We never speak again ... Until I accidentally add Shameplant as a friend on Facebook while writing this story. Oops?

I stare at my phone, confused. Shameplant has accepted my friend request and sent me a message.

What now?!

"
**DUN
DUN
DUN.**
"

CRANBERRY VODKA RETURNS

He's baaack

Hi again.
We've seen him before, haven't we?
I guess everyone deserves a second chance.

CRANBERRY VODKA RETURNS

_____ _____

I HAVEN'T spoken to Cranberry Vodka for a few weeks. Yes, I still talk to him occasionally. OK, maybe more than occasionally.

He calls me on FaceTime singing along to Justin Bieber. I hang up.

He calls me on FaceTime again, still singing along to Justin Bieber. I hang up again.

He calls me on FaceTime a third time. I decline his call.

He never makes time for me, and now he expects me to make time for his phone call? No way. I've spent so much time feeling like I wasn't good enough for him.

A month later, he texts me to ask if I want to grab a drink. I've been upset all week because my best girlfriend is moving away. Since he can always make me laugh, I decide to see him in hopes that it will cheer me up.

We meet at a beach bar a few miles away. He elbows his way to the front and buys two beers and two shots of tequila. He serenades me with a tiny harmonica hanging around his neck and then leads me around the bar, introducing me to every single girl there.

"Hi, this is my friend Tamar. She's looking for friends. You should exchange numbers."

It's awkward but oddly sweet. My face is flushed, and I feel a bit giddy. I exchange uncomfortable goodbyes with a few of the girls at the bar, and we leave.

We end up at his place. I'm sandy from the beach, and he tells me that I have to be clean to sleep in his bed. He puts me in his shower, washes my hair, shaves my legs, and puts me to bed.

The next morning, I vow never to sleep with him again.

"ART MODEL AS IN... NUDE MODEL?"

SPECIMAN
Art teacher/Tutor/Art model, 30 years old, 2 miles away

Artist
Teacher, model
Dancing the night away
Good looking, a little bit naive
Sweet

SPECIMAN

IT'S FIVE MINUTES until midnight on New Year's Eve. I always call an Uber at exactly midnight on NYE to avoid the Uber surcharges, so I'm at the bar, waiting to close out my tab.

The guy next to me looks super familiar, but I can't figure out why. I often see familiar faces from online dating apps when I'm out at bars, so I assume I must have seen him on Tinder.

I turn to him and say, "Hi! You look really familiar. I think maybe I talked to you on Tinder?"

He says, "I've never used online dating, but that's the best pickup line I've ever heard. What's your number?"

I recite my number to him, close out my tab, do a little cheer as the ball drops, and race off to my Uber. Speciman stays to dance with his friends. A few hours later, he texts me, "Hey Tamar, it's Speciman. It would be nice to see you again."

In the morning, I tell him that I would love to see him again. He says he's free most of the week because he doesn't have to go back to work yet.

I type, "What do you do for work?"

"I'm an art teacher, tutor, and art model."

"Art model as in... nude model?"

"Yeah, that's part of the gig!"

I've never met a nude model before. I have so many questions, but I decide to save them for our date.

A few days later, we get together at a bar up the street. I'm still curious about his nude modeling. I ask if I can see his students' drawings of him. At first, he seems kind of weirded out, but then he gets excited as he starts flipping through the various drawings on his phone. Every student's interpretation is slightly different. It looks like he has a nice body ... I start asking questions.

"Is it hard to sit still?"

He takes a sip of his drink, "Yes, it gets pretty boring sometimes. I'm used to it now though."

I cock my head and focus my gaze on him, "Do you feel like you have to stay in better shape?"

"No, I do try to stay in shape, but it's more interesting to draw someone who is older or a bit overweight."

"Have you ever gotten a boner?" I say, very matter-of-factly.

"Haha, no." A smile takes over his face.

"Has anyone drawing you ever gotten a boner?"

His voice squeaks as he says, "Haha, not that I know of." He leans back in his seat, planting his feet into the ground.

I run my finger around the rim of my glass, "Are people allowed to talk to you? How much are you paid per hour? How long do you have to sit there for?"

I think he's flattered by all of my questions. He tells me that he wants to go on another date soon.

The next week, we meet at a hotel bar for a drink. We both order old fashioneds. I ask him if he wants to get food too. He says he's OK, he packed a Tupperware container with dinner in his car.

He brought a tupperware container with food to a date? Is he really low on money? Can he afford these old fashioneds?

I delve into his social life. He says he doesn't really go out, like ever. He has friends, but they hang out at each other's houses, not at bars. It's part of the reason he's single. It's hard to meet people when you never go out. I begin to wonder if we're socially compatible. I bite the inside of my cheek, glancing around the room.

My friends and I go out a lot. I love hanging out at bars, meeting people, and dancing. I ask him if he'd be open to checking out some of my favorite bars, just to try something new. He's never even heard of them!

It's hard to imagine what my life would be like with him. I'm not really at home ever. I'm out at work, out with friends, out working out, or out on a date. I basically only use my apartment to heat up food in the microwave and sleep.

We have a couple cocktails, but I'm getting too drunk. I need to eat dinner and sober up. He walks me to my Uber and kisses me goodnight.

We make plans for another date, although I'm still feeling unsure about how different our social lives are. At the last minute, he asks me if it's OK if we reschedule.

I say, "Yeah, we can reschedule, but I'm not sure if I'm free a single day this week. Possibly Thursday or Sunday. Not sure yet."

He says, "Oh wow, we're two busy people! Let me know. We'll figure something out."

Speciman gets busy with work, and I meet someone else—at a bar, duh—and we both forget to follow up. Missed opportunity?

"

FRANKLY, I'VE BEEN STUCK ON HOW DEMANDING AND CONTROLLING YOU ARE.

"

SAUCEBOX

Chief Technology Officer, 32 years old, 15 miles away

Nerd
Super fit
Straw-like brown hair
OCD but in a chill way
Narcissist

SAUCEBOX

I PLOP ONTO my bed, exhausted from a long workday. Maybe getting promoted wasn't such a good thing after all. I'm going running in an hour, but I need a little break to catch up on my text messages.

Saucebox and I just transitioned from Hinge to texting. We're trying to plan our first date, but we both have impossibly busy schedules. I'm on a work trip, and then he's on a work trip, and then we're both on work trips, and then I'm on a camping trip, and then he has a friend's birthday.

Initially, we plan a date for five weeks away, but then we realize that we will both be in New York at the same time in a couple of weeks. Despite living only fifteen miles apart, our first date is thousands of miles away. I'm looking forward to him canceling six hours before our date though, because such is online dating life, right?

I get home from my work trip in Colorado the week before our date. My boss and I were forced to upgrade our rental car to a convertible because it was the only car available. My boss hates flashy cars. I tell Saucebox about how I kept the top down for the entire two-hour drive.

He jokes, "I'm so jaded from business trips! I barely survive on rental car upgrades, room service, and complimentary snacks."

Work travel can get pretty lonely. I'm excited to have someone to hang out with in New York, even if we don't end up hitting it off.

The week flies by, and before we know it, it's the day of our date. We're on opposite sides of Manhattan, so we meet in the middle at Madison Square.

I'm not that familiar with the subway system, so I elect to walk. It's super humid, and I'm dripping sweat by the time I arrive. Saucebox doesn't seem to notice, but maybe he's being polite. Neither of us knows which restaurant to choose, and we ultimately end up at an overpriced burger joint that serves very strong cocktails.

About thirty minutes into the date, we get into a heated debate about the prevalence of STDs. Saucebox insists that he's terrified of online dating because evil STDs are looming around every corner! I insist that, while he should be careful, he's overreacting, and most things transmitted sexually are curable infections and not diseases. Saucebox asks to see my STD test results, but I haven't been tested in over six months. I typically get tested after every breakup. We continue debating STDs for another hour.

After our date, I have plans to meet up with another friend. Saucebox, like a gentleman, offers to drop me off with his rental car. I only need to travel a couple of miles, but remembering my sweaty walk from earlier, I take him up on his offer. It takes over an hour to traverse two miles. New York traffic makes traffic in my city look like kid stuff. It would have been faster to walk.

Saucebox texts me later that night to try to meet up again, but I opt to continue hanging out with my friend instead.

Back home, I get a text from Saucebox, "What's your schedule looking like this week? We should meet up in the city we actually live in."

Now he suddenly has free time?

Despite our less than stellar first date, I see him a few more times. We go running in the park together, go out to dinner, and then grab drinks at a hipster bar on the other side of town.

As we go on more dates, a few things become very clear:

- ♥ Saucebox is very smart
- ♥ Saucebox knows he's very smart
- ♥ Saucebox thinks everyone else is dumb

Saucebox's "dumb" coworkers become an increasingly frequent topic of conversation. It comes to a head on our fourth and final date.

I manage to get us an invite to the Magic Castle. I may or may not have a connection through a guy I met on Tinder years ago. We both rush to leave work early. I throw on a gown in the bathroom at my office, and he suits up. The Magic Castle has a strict dress code.

We enter on a red carpet and head straight to the bar. My connection is performing that night, so we aren't required to participate in the formal dinner. There are many magicians seated at the bar performing magic tricks for lucky guests. The Castle is dark, with a haunted ambiance. A piano without a pianist plays songs on request. Her name is Myrtle.

I tell Saucebox that I got an STD test, and I was negative for everything.

He takes a gulp of his drink and says, "Did you get tested for herpes?"

"No, my doctor said he doesn't test for it anymore because the test is so inaccurate. There are often false positives." I purse my lips.

"Ugh, that's the only one that I care about, though." He grinds his teeth, glancing around the room.

I sigh deeply and grumble, "Well, I have no reason to believe that I have herpes."

Trying to change the subject, I ask him how his week was, and he launches into a monologue about work and his inept coworkers. I try to point out that his coworkers just have different strengths and weaknesses than he does, but he continues to ramble on. Somewhere around hour two, my eyes glaze over. I wonder how long he can possibly talk about himself. I might as well be a wall. We're missing all of the magic shows.

Three hours in, he reaches into the bar garnish caddy and starts eating the mint leaves that are meant for the cocktails. After the mint leaves, he moves on to the limes, and then the cherries. I watch in horror. I squirm in my seat, feeling a little light-headed.

At the end of four hours, I can't take it anymore. I excuse myself, claiming that I'm tired and need to get to bed. The Magic Castle is closing soon, and we haven't seen a single show.

A few days later, Saucebox texts me that he has decided to renew his lease. He has been toying with the idea of moving to South America since I met him. I panic, thinking that maybe he wants to stay because of me. I tell him that I have to be honest, his negativity towards his coworkers bothers me.

He responds, "Sorry I'm not perfect for you right out of the box today. Frankly, I've been stuck on how demanding and controlling you are. You talk excessively about other men and unload all of your issues onto me."

I wonder when I even had time to unload my issues on him. I point out that he's hardly left room for me to talk about myself, let alone other men. The conversation quickly goes downhill, and we agree to stop seeing one another. To this day, I still haven't met anyone more self-centered.

"

THERE'S AN UBER OUTSIDE WAITING FOR YOU.

"

CRANBERRY VODKA

Again?!

————————————————

But why?
Seriously.
This guy again?
You're better than this, Tamar.

CRANBERRY VODKA

I HAVEN'T SPOKEN to Cranberry Vodka for months. He sends me a poem via text message. I tell him that I want to date him. He tells me that he doesn't have time for a girlfriend.

A month later, he goes on a trip to Vegas with a group of friends. He posts photos every day at the pool with all of the cool kids. There are hot girls in thongs and high heels, good looking men with eight packs, and a photo or two from the DJ stand.

I haven't heard from him all month, but he texts me from the airport to ask when we're going on another date. I know he's at the airport because he always needs attention after a week with his friends. I don't really like them because I don't think they care about him that much, but he seems to enjoy being seen with the coolest guys in the room. Every time I see his best friend he's making out with a different girl.

A couple of weeks go by. I've been asleep for a few hours, when I'm suddenly awoken by a phone call at 2:30 in the morning. I answer, thinking it might be an emergency. It's Cranberry Vodka. He says, "There's an Uber outside waiting for you."

I look outside, and sure enough, there's a car out front. I tell him that I'll come over, but we're not having sex. I'm true to my word.

Deep down, I'm impressed that he had the balls to call an Uber to my apartment, knowing that I would get in. We sleep in until almost 11 a.m. I get goosebumps in the morning as he strokes my cheek. Time seems to slow down to a crawl. I curl up on his belly for a bit and eventually pull myself out of bed. He calls me an Uber home.

The next weekend, I go over to his place and stay the night after going out drinking with my friends. We don't have sex. The weekend after that, I stay over with him again. We don't have sex.

Another week goes by, and another night at his place. We don't have sex.

We start hanging out earlier than 2 a.m., but he will only give me the slots of time that are left over after his time devoted to work, family, and friends. Those time slots are few and far between. He has a lot of friends.

Meanwhile, he expects me to drop everything when he wants to hang out. He refuses to commit to plans in advance or to make an effort to make me a part of his life. I feel like a side chick, and I'm annoyed. I'm holding myself back from meeting better guys by continuing to hang out with him.

I don't understand why he keeps talking to me. He clearly doesn't like me enough to commit. I decide to stop speaking to him.

"DO YOU KNOW WHAT IT MEANS TO BE POLYAMOROUS?"

SWINGRICH

Actor, 35 years old, 3 miles away

Confident
That perfect smile
Always craves attention
Loves being in love, loves working
Drama King
Sagittarius

SWINGRICH

I STARE AT my phone screen, pursing my lips, perplexed. This guy's face looks so familiar. Where do I know him from? I flip through the rest of his photos, searching for a clue. Of course, his fourth photo is him on the set of a popular TV show, in which he has a supporting role. (You know you live in a big city when...)

This has happened to me a lot since I moved here. I see someone that I'm positive I went to college with, but they're actually just another actor. Ugh. Don't get me wrong, I have a great deal of admiration for actors. They audition over and over again, persevering no matter how many times they fail. Failing is hard. Most people can't handle it.

Actors make great friends, and let's be real, most of them are pretty attractive. I've just found that actors often tend to be so focused on getting their careers off the ground that they have little time to invest in a relationship.

Maybe I should give Swingrich a shot, though. He already has some success in his career, so he should be a little less hungry for networking. At the least, he might have some interesting stories.

He invites me to meet him for a sunset walk along the beach, possibly followed by dinner if things go well. I tell him, "Sounds like a plan. See you Thursday!"

He arrives a little late and doesn't look quite as good as his headshots. But he is still attractive, with commanding eye contact, strong posture, and a steady gait. I spend the first hour of the date patiently listening to his speech about his background, career goals, past relationships, family, and hobbies. He hopes to be rich like Jeff Bezos one day.

As the sun creeps below the horizon, I realize that he has yet to ask me a single question about myself. I guess people here really are selfish like people say, including myself. We are so focused on our passions that everything else comes second. He turns to me and asks if I would like to go with him to his favorite dinner spot. I'm starving. What's another hour?

We walk to the place he mentioned. The name seems familiar. I'm imagining a trendy restaurant with unique American food, lots of vegan options, and outdoor patio seating with string lights. To my surprise, we walk up to a … grocery store? Not just any grocery store but the most expensive grocery store that I've ever been inside. My eyes bulge at the price tags.

Swingrich orders salmon, rice, and a coconut with a straw, totaling $28.50. I get the same thing, minus the coconut. We eat around back on a quaint patio with lounge chairs and café tables. It's officially my first-ever date at a grocery store. How romantic.

He stares into my eyes, sipping on his coconut, and says, "I guess I should tell you something about myself."

He takes a deep breath, "Do you know what it means to be polyamorous?"

I lean back and stare at him in silent bewilderment. Isn't that something you should tell someone pre-date rather than one hour in, after you've got them trapped behind a grocery store with a half-eaten salmon?!

He explains that he already has three girlfriends. When he isn't working, he spends all of his time with them. He talks to all three every day. Sounds exhausting. He insists that he's more attentive than most guys who are only seeing one girl.

I'm at a loss for words, so I don't say much of anything. My skin tingles. He keeps going. He tells me all about each of them and how he thinks I would fit in well as lucky number four.

I feel like I've been conned. He asks me out on a second date and I decline, utterly baffled. We conclude our meal in silence. It's the most awkward salmon I've ever eaten. As I try to escape, he leans in to kiss me goodnight. I pull away and walk briskly to my car.

"
I GUESS IT ALL STARTED WITH A DRUG ADDICTION.

"

DILETTANTE

Customer Service Rep, 34 years old, 9 miles away

Hacker
Social, cute
Addictive personality
Fresh out of confinement
Focused

DILETTANTE

I OFTEN GOOGLE my dates before I meet them. I've dug up shocking details hours before a first date. One of my dates was arrested for drug trafficking. One was married. Yet another was registered for multiple MILF dating websites. If I've learned anything, it's that it's always better to know too much going into a date than to be surprised with the details after it's too late.

Dilettante and I are planning our first date, so the time is now. Get ready, Google.

His dating profile only has his first name, with no school or employment information, so I have to dig. It looks like he's a member of a CrossFit gym five miles away. CrossFit gyms always post a lot on Instagram. I look up the gym's Instagram and scroll through the tagged photos. Bingo! I found him! I type his full name into Google, hoping it won't be too hard to locate him.

Whoa. Wait... what? I read the headlines in shock:

"Vengeance Porn Tyrant Pleads Guilty, Faces Nine Years in Prison."

"Local Man in Federal Prison for Vengeance Porn Case."

If I'm doing the math correctly, he only got out of jail a couple of months ago. He didn't waste any time signing up for online dating. I chew at the inside of my cheek, thinking about all of the things that could go wrong if I go on a date with him. I click over to the images tab and find a mugshot, a bathroom selfie, and a picture of Dilettante holding a sign that says he's been sober for four years. I shut my laptop. I can't look at any more right now.

It's been a few hours, and I still haven't responded to Dilettante on Hinge. I left him hanging about our first date. I tell him about what I found on Google. He asks if I will give him a chance to explain. After some thought, I say OK, and we schedule a phone call for the next day. There's no chance anything he has to say will entice me to meet him in person, but I'm dying to hear his explanation.

"Hi! Thanks for calling! Let me step outside. I'm at trivia night with friends," he says jubilantly.

Fresh out of jail and he has enough friends to go to trivia night.

"Where do I begin? I guess it all started with a drug addiction. I was fired from my job because I was always high at work, and I needed money to buy more drugs. I was bored at home, and I hacked a friend's website for fun. Maybe friend is a strong word … He was more of an acquaintance. My acquaintance was so impressed that I was able to hack him that he offered me a job."

I clutch my phone and say, "What was the job?"

"Well, my acquaintance happened to be the founder of a vengeance porn site. He told me that he would pay me a certain amount of money for each photo that I got him. For me at the time, it was a lot of money. I got on Facebook to see if I could get someone to send me a photo, and within twenty minutes I already had one. I started making a lot of money. Like, more than I had ever made before. It was terrible of me, but it was also kind of thrilling. I became addicted to hacking photos. It wasn't about the people in the photos or the stories behind them. It was all about the money and the thrill."

I swallow, biting my lip. "How did you end up in jail?"

He clears his throat and says, "Eventually, the site was busted. It was a real reality check. I was forced to think about the implications of my actions. I had a lot of time in prison to reflect on my experience and how to move forward from it. I realized that I needed to get my life back together. I needed to get sober." *None of this occurred to you until AFTER the site was busted?*

"I want to use my past as fuel for a bright and successful future. I will never make a mistake like that again."

That sounds nice but how can I believe you?

"What have you been doing to improve your life now that you're back home?" I play with a piece of my hair, feeling a little sick to my stomach.

"Well, for starters, I have become very active at my local church. I had never been to church before, but I really love it." Of course. Former drug addicts always seem to become church addicts. At least he's redirecting his addiction to something positive. "That's great! What else have you been up to?"

"I have also met a group of friends through my addiction counseling. I still hang out with my old friends too—that's who I'm at trivia with. My new friends are into Magic the Gathering and Dungeons and Dragons. I can still be around alcohol without drinking, but it's nice to have friends who don't partake in any addictive substances.

Right, they just partake in addictive games instead. I guess being addicted to church and games is better than being addicted to drugs and alcohol though. I tell Dilettante that, unfortunately, I don't think we're compatible. I try to let him down easy and wish him good luck.

LADIES. Google *everyone*.

" I NOTICED THAT YOU DELETED ME ON FACEBOOK. "

CRANBERRY VODKA
The saga continues

Tamar,
he's
just
not
that
into
you.

CRANBERRY VODKA

MY PHONE VIBRATES. I pick it up and see that I have a text from Cranberry Vodka. I immediately open it.

"I need to see you right now."

I roll my eyes and say, "We haven't spoken for like seven months. I have a boyfriend."

"I know. I want a chance to talk before I lose you. I noticed that you deleted me on Facebook."

I sit quietly for an agonizingly long moment and say, "If you meet me outside the bar on my block in thirty minutes, I'll give you an opportunity to talk."

The bar is closed, so we make do with a concrete bench out front. He tells me he's ready to date. I tell him that I can't, I have a boyfriend. He tries to kiss me, and I pull away and walk home.

A couple of days later, I break up with my boyfriend. The next day, I tell Cranberry Vodka. He yells at me for breaking up with my boyfriend. We sort of try to date. It doesn't work out. Is the saga finally over?

A few months later, I have Instacart deliver a Smirnoff ice to his house. I guess I'm not ready for it to be over yet. Truth is, I want what he has to offer. He's unpredictable, hard-working, dedicated to his family, and emotionally strong. He has an understanding of people and how they think and operate, he's easy to get along with, and he always makes me laugh. Unfortunately, he has absolutely no idea what he wants. And let's be real, he just doesn't like me enough. He tells me that he's never flirting with me again.

"
I THOUGHT
IT WOULD
BE WEIRD
TO CRASH
YOUR DATE.
"

KISMET

Software engineer, 29 years old, 1 mile away

Self-involved
Mystery Man
Never met him
Was he worth meeting?
Chance.

KISMET

YES. NO. NO. No. No. Yes. No...

I'm lying in my bed, swiping through Hinge. Kismet messages me and asks if I want to grab a drink some time. He's cute. It looks like he's well-traveled, and he seems laid back. I don't know much about him yet, but so far he's giving off good vibes. We pick a bar to meet at after work next Monday around 7 p.m.

Friday rolls around, and I find myself without plans. Not just any Friday though—it's Valentine's Day. How depressing. My friend from St Louis is in town to see Nelly perform, and she asks if I want to join. Why not? Dancing to throwback music all night seems like a better plan than sitting at home alone. We text a bunch of friends to pull a group together last minute.

We have tickets for the cheap section, so we show up on the earlier side to grab a spot toward the front. We manage to get the last few spots right behind VIP, which is still pretty empty. The DJ is playing 90s songs, so we're content. We sip overpriced beers and wait for the venue to fill up.

After an hour or so of anticipation, Nelly finally emerges on stage. There's this guy in the VIP section wearing a green sweater and a green backwards cap. His sweater looks so familiar for some reason. I can't figure out where I know him from. My friend is like, "Of course you know the guy in front of us. You know someone everywhere we go." He's with a girl, and they have basically been making out nonstop since they arrived. Happy Valentine's day to them.

Nelly's performance reaches its climax, and by this point I've figured out who the guy in the VIP section is. We leave the venue, and as I'm getting in an Uber, I text Kismet. "Is there any chance that you went to the Nelly concert?"

The next morning, he responds, "Haha yeah! Were you there?"

Still lying in bed, I send him a photo of his back. He tells me I should have said hi.

Ummm when though? Was there a five-minute gap when you weren't sucking face?

I say, "Thought it would be weird to crash your date."

He says, "Haha, wouldn't have cared. Wasn't really a date either. Just a friend I met traveling that happened to be in town this week."

Hmmm, just a friend huh?

I contemplate canceling our date. It's just drinks though … What's the harm? It's not like I have other plans on a Monday night.

Monday morning, Kismet texts me and says, "Hey! Still down for drinks later?" Cool, he's not going to cancel the day of, like everyone else. Off to a good start.

After work, I text him saying I'm ready when he is. He says he might be free in the next thirty minutes. Did he forget what time we were supposed to meet?

Two hours later, there is still no word from him. I text him, "Are you ready yet?"

After a long fifteen minutes of staring at my phone waiting for a response, I finally get one: "Was just about to head out from this bar and not sure after. Sorry, that took a little longer than I thought. What are you thinking for tonight?"

So he's at a bar? Getting drinks before we get drinks? I remind him where we decided to meet a week ago.

Another fifteen minutes go by, and Kismet once again fails to answer my text. I try to keep busy around my apartment to distract myself. Finally, I tell him that I'm five minutes away from canceling. I spent Valentine's Day watching him make out with another girl all night, and now he's making me wait around for him. Is this guy even worth meeting?

Seven minutes later, still no response. I cancel the date. On to the next one!

"
I RESPECT HIS WISH TO QUARANTINE, BUT MAYBE I CAN SNEAK OUT ONE NIGHT.
"

RONA

Aspiring Actor/Writer, 30 years old, 14 miles away

So tall
East Coast asshole
Aspiring actor, stock trader
Confident about his perfect pecs
Handsome
Capricorn

RONA

I'M ON MY first-ever FaceTime date. It's no longer considered safe to go out in public, so Rona and I joke that perhaps we will play digital Power Hour. So far, we have just been chatting. Rona is unexpectedly good looking, and he laughs at all my bad jokes. He tells me that I have a great smile. I decide that he's worth meeting in real life.

The next day, I check the news and discover that the governor has issued a mandatory "Safer at Home" order, which requires everyone to work from home until further notice. I scramble to pack up my keyboard, monitor, material samples, notebooks, and drawings sets, unsure how long it will be before I can go back to work. COVID doesn't feel real yet. There is talk around the office that the lockdown might last a month or two, and then everything should go back to normal.

Rona texts me, "Quarantine and chill?" I invite him over. Under normal circumstances, I would never invite a guy to my apartment this early on, but all of the bars and restaurants are closed, and we are only supposed to leave our apartments for essential activities. Technically, even having Rona over is against the rules. I wonder if I could get fined or even arrested. There must be some grace period, right?

Rona knocks on the door. He's so tall that I have to look up to see his face. He's wearing a floral print sweater, and his teeth are perfectly white. Everyone in town is on a first name basis with their dentist, especially those who call themselves "aspiring actors."

We plant ourselves on my couch to get to know one another with a bottle of wine ... or two. He tells me that he moved here from New Jersey a year ago to pursue his dream of becoming an actor. He had made one good connection through an acting class, but it wasn't good enough to save him from working ten hours a day for a stock trading firm. He's living that big city hustle life. He loves his friends here, but they are all sensitive and politically correct. He longs for a few other east coast assholes in his life. (As you should know by now, I kind of have a thing for east coast assholes).

So far in LA, he's only had a series of casual flings. His last serious relationship was back in New Jersey. It ended because his girlfriend accused him of cheating. He says he doesn't want to talk about it, and then he spends the next twenty minutes talking about how he is sure that she cheated on him. He asks if he can stay the night. A little tipsy, I say, "Uhhh sure."

Don't get too excited. Nothing happened.

The next morning, we lay cuddling for a bit. I run my hands through his hair as he massages my shoulders. I fantasize about our future dates. Eventually, we roll out of bed. I'm waiting for him to make some excuse as to why he needs to head home, but instead he pours himself a glass of water and sits on the couch, scrolling through his text messages. I start to fry eggs and bacon, and he butters some bread and brews a pot of coffee.

We finish cooking, eat our breakfast, and then he asks if I want to watch a movie. He is clearly not planning on leaving any time soon. He grabs another bottle of wine and heads to the couch. Turns out when he said, "Quarantine and chill?" he wasn't kidding.

After the movie ends, my sister is bored at home and texts me to see if I want to play solitaire over Zoom. Rona is meeting my family on our first date. We've already broken most of the first date rules, so why not?

We play for an hour and then log off to do something else. We purchase a Jackbox TV party pack, but when we try to play, we discover that all of the games require three players minimum. We set up a GoTo Meeting to screenshare and call up my friend to join us. She's at home bored too. We start playing, and Rona grabs another bottle of wine. It's kind of weird that Rona doesn't even know what my friend looks like, and yet here we are playing digital games together.

Since I made breakfast, Rona orders dinner for us on Postmates. Twenty-two hours in, still going strong. After dinner, we head to my room for a cuddling session. Rona starts to ask if he can stay over a second night, but then he pulls up his work email. He scrolls through about twenty unread emails and says, "I should go home." Solid twenty-six-hour first date.

The next evening, Rona asks if I want to come over and watch a movie. I'm still in my pajamas. I've been working from home all day. I hop in the shower and then head over to his place. I wonder if his roommates have been washing their hands and if I could get pulled over for leaving my apartment. I'm the only car on the freeway.

After the movie, I stay the night. Maybe my car will stand out less if I leave when essential employees are going to work in the morning. It's nice to have physical contact when everyone is so isolated, but he coughs a few times throughout the night. I wonder if I'm making a mistake.

In the morning, the freeway is still empty. The city feels like a ghost town. Rona sends me COVID memes all day. I ask him if he wants to come by for dinner.

He says, "Of course!" He arrives in sweatpants with disheveled hair. He hasn't showered. The chase is over, I guess.

I cook pretzel-crusted chicken and broccoli, and he tells me about a big fight he had with his roommates. Both of his roommates were laid off from their jobs, and it's challenging for him to be the only one at home working. He's not used to spending so much time with them. Everything they do grates at his nerves—the way his roommate opens the cabinets, the way his roommate does (or doesn't) do the dishes, and the smell of the food that his roommate cooks. One of them has been sleeping with a different guy every night, and it's making his other roommate uncomfortable. She could bring COVID into the house.

A couple of days later, Rona texts me a selfie. He's waiting in line at a grocery store with a shirt tied around his face. Apparently, we're supposed to wear masks in public now. He invites me to come over after work and sit on his back porch. I leave during rush hour, and the freeway is still empty. It's eerie. I make it across town in a quarter of the amount of time that it normally takes.

We share a bottle of wine and gaze at the stars, and then I stay the night. More coughing. What if he gets me sick? Is it worth risking my life over a guy I barely know? It's so lonely at my apartment, though, all by myself. My friends all have families or roommates or boyfriends. I'm at home all alone.

The weekend comes and goes, and I don't see Rona at all. Sunday night, Rona sends me a picture of himself gardening. He's shirtless, and he's holding a shovel at a weird angle that makes his arms look good. I roll my eyes and text, "LOL."

I don't hear from Rona at all for a few days, and then late Wednesday night he texts me, "Work was crazy this week. I was logging out at 8:30-9ish every day. Probably the same for next week."I type, "Oh nooo, I guess it's better than being unemployed, though. How are things with your roommates?"

"My roommate knocked on my door and woke me yesterday because he was delivering a mask to his girlfriend's place. LOL. I guess he needs to know where we are at all times."

A couple of days later, Rona finally comes over for dinner and a movie. He stays the night. After he leaves, I don't hear from him for a few days. I text him to check in. He says, "I wanna come over."

"You can if you want. Or are you not allowed?"

"Yea, we had a talk, and we are doing a strict two-week quarantine. My roommate is taking all of the necessary precautions, and I've just been going out doing my own thing. It's not right to him. I respect his wish to quarantine, but maybe I can sneak out one night."

"Well, you're welcome to sneak out and come here. I don't feel like it's adding much threat given that we've been seeing each other for over two weeks, and I'm not seeing anyone else. I get it if you don't want to defy your roommate, though."

"It's not so much defying as it is respecting his wishes, because I know if I had an issue with something, he'd be the same. But yeah, I'll let you know."

Two weeks go by, and I don't see him. I text Rona to see if he had another talk with his roommates. He says he's avoiding the conversation, but that he's been tracking his roommate's habits throughout the day, and has figured out that he leaves his room at about the same times each day. His other roommate offered to cover for him if he wants to sneak out. He says he will try to sneak out one day this week.

A few days later, Rona knocks on my door. He has to leave by 6:00 a.m. so that he's home before his cautious roommate wakes up. Afterward, Rona goes quiet again. He never texts me first. Sometimes I reach out to him, but I always end up consoling him about work. He never asks about my day. I'm having trouble falling asleep at night, and I feel a little bitter every time I think about him. I'm tired of being the only one to reach out. Is it worth seeing a guy who doesn't make time for me when we have nothing but free time?

I text him and tell him that I'm going to find a new quarantine buddy. He says he understands and asks if we can remain friends. I say, "Of course."

We never speak again.

"I'M READY TO HAVE A GIRLFRIEND."

CRANBERRY VODKA

One more for the road

Until
next
time

CRANBERRY VODKA

THE SAFER at Home order has been in effect for a couple of months. Cranberry Vodka's friend gets coronavirus and passes away, so I send him a funny story to cheer him up. He tells me he's ready to have a girlfriend. We talk for twenty-four hours, and then he loses interest. We haven't spoken since.

EPILOGUE

FIRST THINGS FIRST—I would LOVE to hear about your bad date stories. Please share your stories at **saltyflamesthebook@gmail.com.** Now, most of you are probably wondering if I ever found mutual love. I am delighted to announce that I have been happily taken since shortly after I last spoke to Cranberry Vodka. (And not by Cranberry Vodka.) I'm not going to share the story, because life isn't about an end destination. Life is a journey, and I have no regrets for all of the terrible dates that I went on. In writing these stories, I looked up all of the guys on social media, and most of them are happily taken as well. Everyone has their person. They just weren't mine. I wouldn't be the person I am today if it weren't for these experiences. So start swiping. At the very least, you will end up with a few good stories.

ACKNOWLEDGMENTS

My sister, for helping design my book and helping to get my idea off the ground.

My editor, Alessandor, for making me sound like a writer.

My mom, for reassuring me that it's OK to go on thirty first dates (x5 or so).

My friends, for reading my stories and providing constant encouragement.

My roommates, for patiently listening to me talk nonstop about my book and for providing support and ideas.

My boyfriend, for reminding me to buy a book on writing a book and for, without complaint, giving up hours and hours of time that we could have spent together so that I could write about other men.

SPARK Publications, for making my book legit.

Last but not least, thank you to the men who provided content for this book. It didn't work out, but you have provided a lifetime of lessons and stories that I will forever look back on with laughs and fond memories. I truly wish the best for all of you. It wasn't you; it was me.

ABOUT THE AUTHOR

TAMAR TREMAINE is an architect with a side job as a professional online dater. She's been on hundreds of first dates and chatted online with thousands of men. On a few occasions, she's been on as many as three dates in one day. She went to a few great universities and won a few awards. In elementary school, she was selected out of hundreds of students for the "Optimist" award. This is her first book. She doesn't consider herself an author but rather a normal person with a lot of great stories to tell. Tamar hopes to inspire you to put yourself out there, download that app, go on that date, and call that guy back. After all, what's the worst that could happen?

CHECK OUT TAMAR TREMAINE ON SOCIAL MEDIA!

@saltyflamesthebook   /saltyflamesthebook

CPSIA information can be obtained
at www.ICGtesting.com
Printed in the USA
BVHW051412070921
616209BV00017B/679